The Boor, a Comedy in One Act

By Anton Pavlovich Chekhov

Layout and Cover Copyright ©2014
All Rights Reserved

Table of Contents

Persons in the Play 4

The Boor 5

Persons in the Play

HELENA IVANOVNA POPOV, a young widow, mistress of a country estate

GRIGORI STEPANOVITCH SMIRNOV, proprietor of a country estate

LUKA, servant of MRS. POPOV

A gardener. A Coachman. Several workmen.

The Boor

TIME: The present.

SCENE: A well-furnished reception-room in MRS. POPOV'S home. MRS. POPOV is discovered in deep mourning, sitting upon a sofa, gazing steadfastly at a photograph. LUKA is also present.

LUKA: It isn't right, ma'am. You're wearing yourself out! The maid and the cook have gone looking for berries; everything that breathes is enjoying life; even the cat knows how to be happy—slips about the courtyard and catches birds—but you hide yourself here in the house as though you were in a cloister. Yes, truly, by actual reckoning you haven't left this house for a whole year.

MRS. POPOV: And I shall never leave it—why should I? My life is over. He lies in his grave, and I have buried myself within these four walls. We are both dead.

LUKA: There you are again! It's too awful to listen to, so it is! Nikolai Michailovitch is dead; it was the will of the Lord, and the Lord has given him eternal peace. You have grieved over it and that ought to be enough. Now it's time to stop. One can't weep and wear mourning forever! My wife died a few years ago. I grieved for her. I wept a whole month—and then it was over. Must one be forever singing lamentations? That would be more than your husband was worth! [He sighs.] You have forgotten all your neighbors. You don't go out and you receive no one. We live—you'll pardon me—like the spiders, and the good light of day we never see. All the livery is eaten by mice—as though there weren't any more nice people in the world! But the whole neighborhood is full of gentlefolk. The regiment is stationed in Riblov—officers—simply beautiful! One can't see enough of them! Every Friday a ball, and military music every day. Oh, my dear, dear ma'am, young and pretty as you are, if you'd only let your spirits live—! Beauty can't last forever. When ten short years are over, you'll be glad enough to go out a bit and meet the officers—and then it'll be too late.

MRS. POPOV: [Resolutely.] Please don't speak of these things again. You know very well that since the death of Nikolai Michailovitch my life is absolutely nothing to me. You think I live, but it only seems so. Do you understand? Oh, that his departed soul may see how I love him! I know, it's no secret to you; he was often unjust to me, cruel, and—he wasn't faithful, but I shall be faithful to the grave and prove to him how I can love. There, in the Beyond, he'll find me the same as I was until his death.

LUKA: What is the use of all these words, when you'd so much rather go walking in the garden or order Tobby or Welikan harnessed to the trap, and visit the neighbors?

MRS. POPOV: [Weeping.] Oh!

LUKA: Madam, dear madam, what is it? In Heaven's name!

MRS. POPOV: He loved Tobby so! He always drove him to the Kortschagins or the Vlassovs. What a wonderful horseman he was! How fine he looked when he pulled at the reigns with all his might! Tobby, Tobby—give him an extra measure of oats to-day!

LUKA: Yes, ma'am.

[A bell rings loudly.]

MRS. POPOV: [Shudders.] What's that? I am at home to no one.

LUKA: Yes, ma'am.

[He goes out, centre.]

MRS. POPOV: [Gazing at the photograph.] You shall see, Nikolai, how I can love and forgive! My love will die only with me—when my poor heart stops beating.

[She smiles through her tears.] And aren't you ashamed? I have been a good, true wife; I have imprisoned myself and I shall remain true until death, and you—you—you're not ashamed of yourself, my dear monster! You quarrelled with me, left me alone for weeks—

[LUKA enters in great excitement.]

LUKA: Oh, ma'am, someone is asking for you, insists on seeing you—

MRS. POPOV: You told him that since my husband's death I receive no one?

LUKA: I said so, but he won't listen; he says it is a pressing matter.

MRS. POPOV: I receive no one!

LUKA: I told him that, but he's a wild man; he swore and pushed himself into the room; he's in the dining-room now.

MRS. POPOV: [Excitedly.] Good. Show him in. The impudent—!

[LUKA goes out, centre.]

MRS. POPOV: What a bore people are! What can they want with me? Why do they disturb my peace? [She sighs.] Yes, it is clear I must enter a convent. [Meditatively.] Yes, a convent.

[SMIRNOV enters, followed by LUKA.]

SMIRNOV: [To LUKA.] Fool, you make too much noise! You're an ass! [Discovering MRS. POPOV—politely.] Madam, I have the honor to introduce myself: Lieutenant in the Artillery, retired, country gentleman, Grigori Stapanovitch Smirnov! I'm compelled to bother you about an exceedingly important matter.

MRS. POPOV: [Without offering her hand.] What is it you wish?

SMIRNOV: Your deceased husband, with whom I had the honor to be acquainted, left me two notes amounting to about twelve hundred roubles. Inasmuch as I have to pay the interest to-morrow on a loan from the Agrarian Bank, I should like to request, madam, that you pay me the money to-day.

MRS. POPOV: Twelve-hundred—and for what was my husband indebted to you?

SMIRNOV: He bought oats from me.

MRS. POPOV: [With a sigh, to LUKA.] Don't forget to give Tobby an extra measure of oats.

[LUKA goes out.]

MRS. POPOV: [To SMIRNOV.] If Nikolai Michailovitch is indebted to you, I shall, of course, pay you, but I am sorry, I haven't the money to-day. To-morrow my manager will return from the city and I shall notify him to pay you what is due you, but until then I cannot satisfy your request. Furthermore, today is just seven months since the death of my husband, and I am not in the mood to discuss money matters.

SMIRNOV: And I am in the mood to fly up the chimney with my feet in the air if I can't lay hands on that interest to-morrow. They'll seize my estate!

MRS. POPOV: Day after to-morrow you will receive the money.

SMIRNOV: I don't need the money day after to-morrow; I need it to-day.

MRS. POPOV: I'm sorry I can't pay you today.

SMIRNOV: And I can't wait until day after to-morrow.

MRS. POPOV: But what can I do if I haven't it?

SMIRNOV: So you can't pay?

MRS. POPOV: I cannot.

SMIRNOV: Hm! Is that your last word?

MRS. POPOV: My last.

SMIRNOV: Absolutely?

MRS. POPOV: Absolutely.

SMIRNOV: Thank you. [He shrugs his shoulders.] And they expect me to stand for all that. The toll-gatherer just now met me in the road and asked why I was always worrying. Why, in Heaven's name, shouldn't I worry? I need money, I feel the knife at my throat. Yesterday morning I left my house in the early dawn and called on all my debtors. If even one of them had paid his debt! I worked the skin off my fingers! The devil knows in what sort of Jew-inn I slept; in a room with a barrel of brandy! And now at last I come here, seventy versts from home, hope for a little money, and all you give me is moods! Why shouldn't I worry?

MRS. POPOV: I thought I made it plain to you that my manager will return from town, and then you will get your money.

SMIRNOV: I did not come to see the manager; I came to see you. What the devil—pardon the language—do I care for your manager?

MRS. POPOV: Really, sir, I am not used to such language or such manners. I shan't listen to you any further.

[She goes out, left.]

SMIRNOV: What can one say to that? Moods! Seven months since her husband died! Do I have to pay the interest or not? I repeat the question, have I to pay the interest or not? The husband is dead and all that; the manager is—the devil with him!—travelling somewhere. Now, tell me, what am I to do? Shall I run away from my creditors in a balloon? Or knock my head against a stone wall? If I call on Grusdev he chooses to be "not at home," Iroschevitch has simply hidden himself, I have quarrelled with Kurzin and came near throwing him out of the window, Masutov is ill and this woman has—moods! Not one of them will pay up! And all because I've spoiled them, because I'm an old whiner, dish-rag! I'm too tender-hearted with them. But wait! I allow nobody to play tricks with me, the devil with 'em all! I'll stay here and not budge until she pays! Brr! How angry I am, how terribly angry I am! Every tendon is trembling with anger, and I can hardly breathe! I'm even growing ill! [He calls out.] Servant!

[LUKA enters.]

LUKA: What is it you wish?

SMIRNOV: Bring me Kvas or water! [LUKA goes out.] Well, what can we do? She hasn't it on hand? What sort of logic is that? A fellow stands with the knife at his throat, he needs money, he is on the point of hanging himself, and she won't pay because she isn't in the mood to discuss money matters. Women's logic! That's why I never liked to talk to women, and why I dislike doing it now. I would rather sit on a powder barrel than talk with a woman. Brr!—I'm getting cold as ice; this affair has made me so angry. I need only to see such a romantic creature from a distance to get so angry that I have cramps in my calves! It's enough to make one yell for help!

[Enter LUKA.]

LUKA: [Hands him water.] Madam is ill and is not receiving.

SMIRNOV: March! [LUKA goes out.] Ill and isn't receiving! All right, it isn't necessary. I won't receive, either! I'll sit here and stay until you bring that money. If you're ill a week, I'll sit here a week. If you're ill a year, I'll sit here a year. As Heaven is my witness, I'll get the money. You don't disturb me with your mourning—or with your dimples. We know these dimples! [He calls out the window.] Simon, unharness! We aren't going to leave right away. I am going to stay here. Tell them in the stable to give the horses some oats. The left horse has twisted the bridle again. [Imitating him.] Stop! I'll show you how. Stop! [Leaves window.] It's awful. Unbearable heat, no money, didn't sleep last night and now—mourning-dresses with moods. My head aches; perhaps I ought to have a drink. Ye-s, I must have a drink. [Calling.] Servant!

LUKA: What do you wish?

SMIRNOV: Something to drink! [LUKA goes out. SMIRNOV sits down and looks at his clothes.] Ugh, a fine figure! No use denying that. Dust, dirty boots, unwashed, uncombed, straw on my vest—the lady probably took me for a highwayman. [He yawns.] It was a little impolite to come into a reception-room with such clothes. Oh, well, no harm done. I'm not here as a guest. I'm a creditor. And there is no special costume for creditors.

LUKA: [Entering with glass.] You take great liberty, sir.

SMIRNOV: [Angrily.] What?

LUKA: I—I—I just——

SMIRNOV: Whom are you talking to? Keep quiet.

LUKA: [Angrily.] Nice mess! This fellow won't leave!

[He goes out.]

SMIRNOV: Lord, how angry I am! Angry enough to throw mud at the whole world! I even feel ill! Servant!

[MRS. POPOV comes in with downcast eyes.]

MRS. POPOV: Sir, in my solitude I have become unaccustomed to the human voice and I cannot stand the sound of loud talking. I beg you, please to cease disturbing my rest.

SMIRNOV: Pay me my money and I'll leave.

MRS. POPOV: I told you once, plainly, in your native tongue, that I haven't the money at hand; wait until day after to-morrow.

SMIRNOV: And I also had the honor of informing you in your native tongue that I need the money, not day after to-morrow, but to-day. If you don't pay me to-day I shall have to hang myself to-morrow.

MRS. POPOV: But what can I do if I haven't the money?

SMIRNOV: So you are not going to pay immediately? You're not?

MRS. POPOV: I cannot.

SMIRNOV: Then I'll sit here until I get the money. [He sits down.] You will pay day after to-morrow? Excellent! Here I stay until day after to-morrow. [Jumps up.] I ask you, do I have to pay that interest to-morrow or not? Or do you think I'm joking?

MRS. POPOV: Sir, I beg of you, don't scream! This is not a stable.

SMIRNOV: I'm not talking about stables, I'm asking you whether I have to pay that interest to-morrow or not?

MRS. POPOV: You have no idea how to treat a lady.

SMIRNOV: Oh, yes, I have.

MRS. POPOV: No, you have not. You are an ill-bred, vulgar person! Respectable people don't speak so to ladies.

SMIRNOV: How remarkable! How do you want one to speak to you? In French, perhaps! Madame, je vous prie! Pardon me for having disturbed you. What beautiful weather we are having to-day! And how this mourning becomes you!

[He makes a low bow with mock ceremony.]

MRS. POPOV: Not at all funny! I think it vulgar!

SMIRNOV: [Imitating her.] Not at all funny—vulgar! I don't understand how to behave in the company of ladies. Madam, in the course of my life I have seen more women than you have sparrows. Three times have I fought duels for women, twelve I jilted and nine jilted me. There was a time when I played the fool, used honeyed language, bowed and scraped. I loved, suffered, sighed to the moon, melted in love's torments. I loved passionately, I loved to madness, loved in every key, chattered like a magpie on emancipation, sacrificed half my fortune in the tender passion, until now the devil knows I've had enough of it. Your obedient servant will let you lead him around by the nose no more. Enough! Black eyes, passionate eyes, coral lips, dimples in cheeks, moonlight whispers, soft, modest sights—for all that, madam, I wouldn't pay a kopeck! I am not speaking of present company, but of women in general; from the tiniest to the greatest, they are conceited, hypocritical, chattering, odious, deceitful from top to toe; vain, petty, cruel with a maddening logic and [he strikes his forehead] in this respect, please excuse my frankness, but one sparrow is worth ten of the aforementioned petticoat-philosophers. When one sees one of the romantic creatures before him he imagines he is looking at some holy being, so wonderful that its one breath could dissolve him in a sea of a thousand charms and delights; but if one looks into the soul—it's nothing but a common crocodile. [He siezes the arm-chair and breaks it in two.] But the worst of all is that this crocodile imagines it is a masterpiece of creation, and that it has a monopoly on all the tender passions. May the devil hang me upside down if there is anything to love about a woman! When she is in love, all she knows is how to complain and shed tears. If the man suffers and makes sacrifices she swings her train about and tries to lead him by the nose. You have the misfortune to be a woman, and naturally you know woman's nature; tell me on your honor, have you ever in your life seen a woman who was really true and faithful? Never! Only the old and the deformed are true and faithful. It's easier to find a cat with horns or a white woodcock, than a faithful woman.

MRS. POPOV: But allow me to ask, who is true and faithful in love? The man, perhaps?

SMIRNOV: Yes, indeed! The man!

MRS. POPOV: The man! [She laughs sarcastically.] The man true and faithful in love! Well, that is something new! [Bitterly.] How can you make such a statement? Men true and faithful! So long as we have gone thus far, I may as well say that of all the men I have known, my husband was the best; I loved him passionately with all my soul, as only a young, sensible woman may love; I gave him my youth, my happiness, my fortune, my life. I worshipped him like a heathen. And what happened? This best of men betrayed me in every possible way. After his death I found his desk filled with love-letters. While he was alive he left me alone for months—it is horrible even to think about it—he made love to other women in my very presence, he wasted my money and made fun of my feelings—and in spite of everything I trusted him and was true to him. And more than that: he is dead and I am still true to him. I have buried myself within these four walls and I shall wear this mourning to my grave.

SMIRNOV: [Laughing disrespectfully.] Mourning! What on earth do you take me for? As if I didn't know why you wore this black domino and why you buried yourself within these four walls. Such a secret! So romantic! Some knight will pass the castle, gaze up at the windows, and think to himself: "Here dwells the mysterious Tamara who, for love of her husband, has buried herself within four walls." Oh, I understand the art!

MRS. POPOV: [Springing up.] What? What do you mean by saying such things to me?

SMIRNOV: You have buried yourself alive, but meanwhile you have not forgotten to powder your nose!

MRS. POPOV: How dare you speak so?

SMIRNOV: Don't scream at me, please; I'm not the manager. Allow me to call things by their right names. I am not a woman, and I am accustomed to speak out what I think. So please don't scream.

MRS. POPOV: I'm not screaming. It is you who are screaming. Please leave me, I beg you.

SMIRNOV: Pay me my money, and I'll leave.

MRS. POPOV: I won't give you the money.

SMIRNOV: You won't? You won't give me my money?

MRS. POPOV: I don't care what you do. You won't get a kopeck! Leave me!

SMIRNOV: As I haven't had the pleasure of being either your husband or your fiancé, please don't make a scene. [He sits down.] I can't stand it.

MRS. POPOV: [Breathing hard.] You are going to sit down?

SMIRNOV: I already have.

MRS. POPOV: Kindly leave the house!

SMIRNOV: Give me the money.

MRS. POPOV: I don't care to speak with impudent men. Leave! [Pause.] You aren't going?

SMIRNOV: No.

MRS. POPOV: No?

SMIRNOV: No.

MRS. POPOV: Very well.

[She rings the bell. Enter LUKA.]

MRS. POPOV: Luka, show the gentleman out.

LUKA: [Going to SMIRNOV.] Sir, why don't you leave when you are ordered? What do you want?

SMIRNOV: [Jumping up.] Whom do you think you are talking to? I'll grind you to powder.

LUKA: [Puts his hand to his heart.] Good Lord! [He drops into a chair.] Oh, I'm ill; I can't breathe!

MRS. POPOV: Where is Dascha? [Calling.] Dascha! Pelageja! Dascha!

[She rings.]

LUKA: They're all gone! I'm ill! Water!

MRS. POPOV: [To SMIRNOV.] Leave! Get out!

SMIRNOV: Kindly be a little more polite!

MRS. POPOV: [Striking her fists and stamping her feet.] You are vulgar! You're a boor! A monster!

SMIRNOV: What did you say?

MRS. POPOV: I said you were a boor, a monster!

SMIRNOV: [Steps toward her quickly.] Permit me to ask what right you have to insult me?

MRS. POPOV: What of it? Do you think I am afraid of you?

SMIRNOV: And you think that because you are a romantic creature you can insult me without being punished? I challenge you!

LUKA: Merciful Heaven! Water!

SMIRNOV: We'll have a duel!

MRS. POPOV: Do you think because you have big fists and a steer's neck I am afraid of you?

SMIRNOV: I allow no one to insult me, and I make no exception because you are a woman, one of the "weaker sex!"

MRS. POPOV: [Trying to cry him down.] Boor, boor, boor!

SMIRNOV: It is high time to do away with the old superstition that it is only the man who is forced to give satisfaction. If there is equity at all let their be equity in all things. There's a limit!

MRS. POPOV: You wish to fight a duel? Very well.

SMIRNOV: Immediately.

MRS. POPOV: Immediately. My husband had pistols. I'll bring them. [She hurries away, then turns.] Oh, what a pleasure it will be to put a bullet in your impudent head. The devil take you!

[She goes out.]

SMIRNOV: I'll shoot her down! I'm no fledgling, no sentimental young puppy. For me there is no weaker sex!

LUKA: Oh, sir. [Falls to his knees.] Have mercy on me, an old man, and go away. You have frightened me to death already, and now you want to fight a duel.

SMIRNOV: [Paying no attention.] A duel. That's equity, emancipation. That way the sexes are made equal. I'll shoot her down as a matter of principle. What can a person say to such a woman? [Imitating her.] "The devil take you. I'll put a bullet in your impudent head." What can one say to that? She was angry, her eyes blazed, she accepted the challenge. On my honor, it's the first time in my life that I ever saw such a woman.

LUKA: Oh, sir. Go away. Go away!

SMIRNOV: That is a woman. I can understand her. A real woman. No shilly-shallying, but fire, powder, and noise! It would be a pity to shoot a woman like that.

LUKA: [Weeping.] Oh, sir, go away.

[Enter MRS. POPOV.]

MRS. POPOV: Here are the pistols. But before we have our duel, please show me how to shoot. I have never had a pistol in my hand before!

LUKA: God be merciful and have pity upon us! I'll go and get the gardener and the coachman. Why has this horror come to us?

[He goes out.]

SMIRNOV: [Looking at the pistols.] You see, there are different kinds. There are special duelling pistols, with cap and ball. But these are revolvers, Smith & Wesson, with ejectors; fine pistols! A pair like that cost at least ninety roubles. This is the way to hold a revolver. [Aside.] Those eyes, those eyes! A real woman!

MRS. POPOV: Like this?

SMIRNOV: Yes, that way. Then you pull the hammer back—so—then you aim—put your head back a little. Just stretch your arm out, please. So—then press your finger on the thing like that, and that is all. The chief thing is this: don't get excited, don't hurry your aim, and take care that your hand doesn't tremble.

MRS. POPOV: It isn't well to shoot inside; let's go into the garden.

SMIRNOV: Yes. I'll tell you now, I am going to shoot into the air.

MRS. POPOV: That is too much! Why?

SMIRNOV: Because——because. That's my business.

MRS. POPOV: You are afraid. Yes. A-h-h-h. No, no, my dear sir, no flinching! Please follow me. I won't rest until I've made a hole in that head I hate so much. Are you afraid?

SMIRNOV: Yes, I'm afraid.

MRS. POPOV: You are lying. Why won't you fight?

SMIRNOV: Because—because—I—like you.
MRS. POPOV: [With an angry laugh.] You like me! He dares to say he likes me! [She points to the door.] Go.

SMIRNOV: [Laying the revolver silently on the table, takes his hat and starts. At the door he stops a moment, gazing at her silently, then he approaches her, hesitating.] Listen! Are you still angry? I was mad as the devil, but please understand me—how can I express myself? The thing is like this—such things are— [He raises his voice.] Now, is it my fault that you owe me money? [Grasps the back of the chair, which breaks.] The devil know what breakable furniture you have! I like you! Do you understand? I—I'm almost in love!

MRS. POPOV: Leave! I hate you.

SMIRNOV: Lord! What a woman! I never in my life met one like her. I'm lost, ruined! I've been caught like a mouse in a trap.

MRS. POPOV: Go, or I'll shoot.

SMIRNOV: Shoot! You have no idea what happiness it would be to die in sight of those beautiful eyes, to die from the revolver in this little velvet hand! I'm mad! Consider it and decide immediately, for if I go now, we shall never see each other again. Decide—speak—I am a noble, a respectable man, have an income of ten thousand, can shoot a coin thrown into the air. I own some fine horses. Will you be my wife?

MRS. POPOV: [Swings the revolver angrily.] I'll shoot!

SMIRNOV: My mind is not clear—I can't understand. Servant—water! I have fallen in love like any young man. [He takes her hand and she cries with pain.] I love you! [He kneels.] I love you as I have never loved before. Twelve women I jilted, nine jilted me, but not one of them all have I loved as I love you. I am conquered, lost; I lie at your feet like a fool and beg for your hand. Shame and disgrace! For five years I haven't been in love; I thanked the Lord for it, and now I am caught, like a carriage tongue in another carriage. I beg for your hand! Yes or no? Will you?—Good!

[He gets up and goes quickly to the door.]

MRS. POPOV: Wait a minute!

SMIRNOV: [Stopping.] Well?

MRS. POPOV: Nothing. You may go. But—wait a moment. No, go on, go on. I hate you. Or—no; don't go. Oh, if you knew how angry I was, how angry! [She throws the revolver on to the chair.] My finger is swollen from this thing. [She angrily tears her handkerchief.] What are you standing there for? Get out!

SMIRNOV: Farewell!

MRS. POPOV: Yes, go. [Cries out.] Why are you going? Wait—no, go!! Oh, how angry I am! Don't come too near, don't come too near—er—come—no nearer.

SMIRNOV: [Approaching her.] How angry I am with myself! Fall in love like a schoolboy, throw myself on my knees. I've got a chill! [Strongly.] I love you. This is fine—all I needed was to fall in love. To-morrow I have to pay my interest, the hay harvest has begun, and then you appear! [He takes her in his arms.] I can never forgive myself.

MRS. POPOV: Go away! Take your hands off me! I hate you—you—this is—

[A long kiss. Enter LUKA with an axe, the gardener with a rake, the coachman with a pitchfork, and workmen with poles.]

LUKA: [Staring at the pair.] Merciful heavens!

[A long pause.]

MRS. POPOV: [Dropping her eyes.] Tell them in the stable that Tobby isn't to have any oats.

CURTAIN

CPSIA information can be obtained
at www.ICGtesting.com
Printed in the USA
LVHW011147071222
734696LV00003BA/629